How to read a city map

How to read a city map

BY DOROTHY RHODES

Photography and Cartography by Aerial Surveying and Engineering Co.

AN ELK GROVE BOOK

CHILDRENS PRESS, CHICAGO

To read a map you need to know that a map can show something large...

(This is a "bird's-eye view")

made smaller...   and smaller...   and even smaller...

4

And very much
smaller until it is one
of many things shown
on a map.

This is the symbol for
a school. The flag
shows that it is an
elementary school.

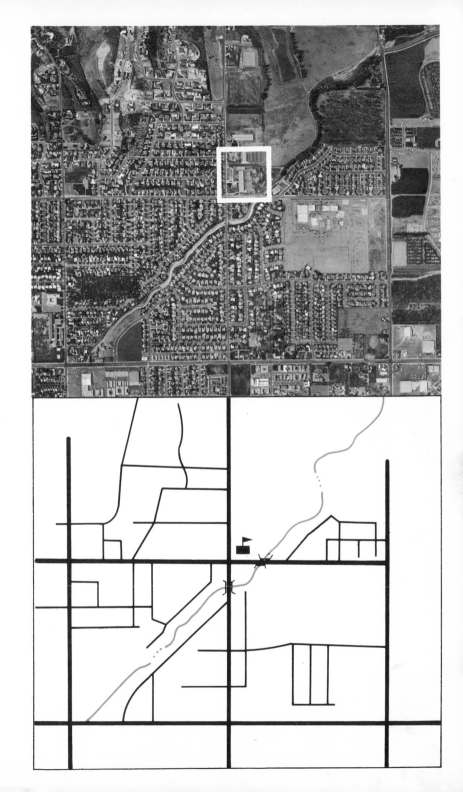

A map can show

a whole city!

A map can show

streets that are straight   streets that curve.

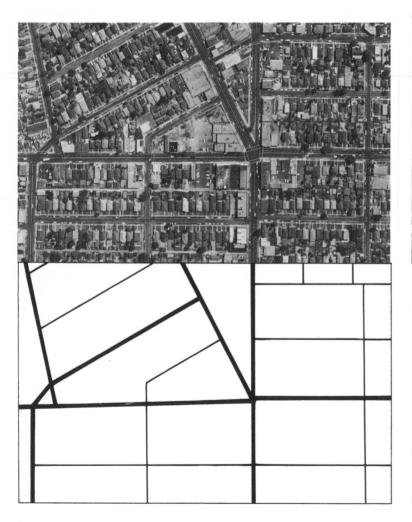

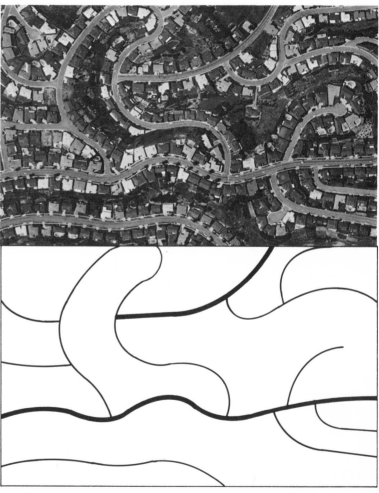

You can tell from a map where
streets cross one another.

This is called an intersection.

(Can you find any schools on this map?)

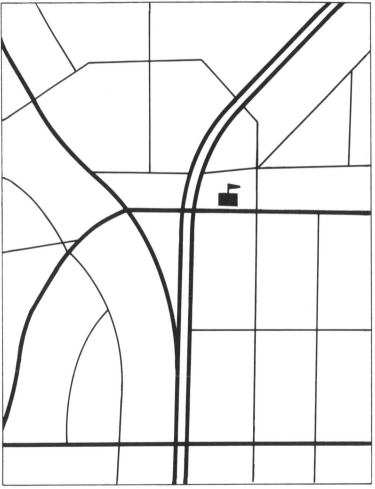

9

Maps use lines and colors to give more facts about streets and roads.

(Do you know what any of these lines mean?)

—————————————————— shows a regular city street.

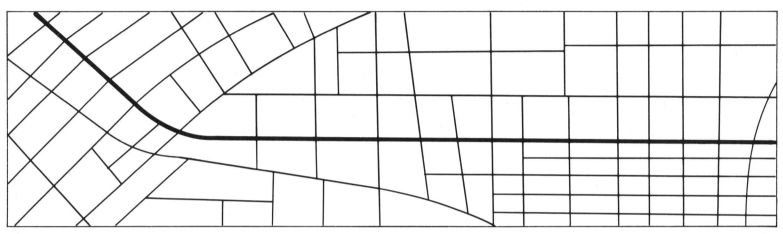

(Do you see any streets that curve?)

It may have 2 or 4 lanes. It is probably like the street you

live on. Most of the streets in a town or city are this kind.

A city map shows straight or curved streets.

This thick black line stands for a street that is wide. It may go through a shopping center. Many cars will use this street. Traffic lights will signal stop and go.

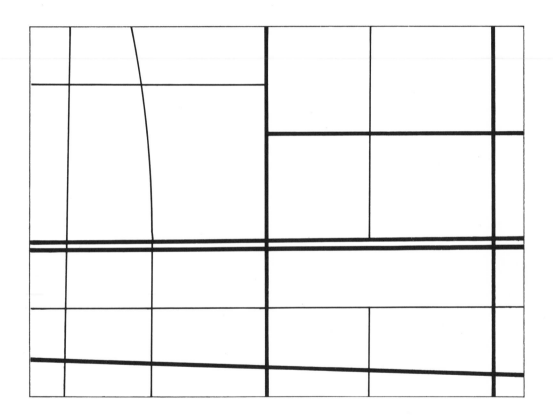

(Can you find the wide streets on this map? Can you find a wide street that is divided?)

This is a map

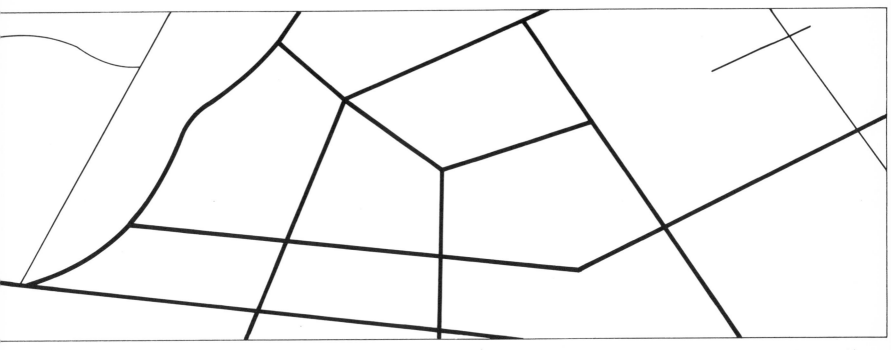

(Why are there so many wide, black lines on the map?)

of this:

This tells you

the road is a freeway.

_____

There are no traffic lights on it.

The traffic does not have to stop

for red lights.

(Can you find where the freeway is divided? ▬▬▬ *)*

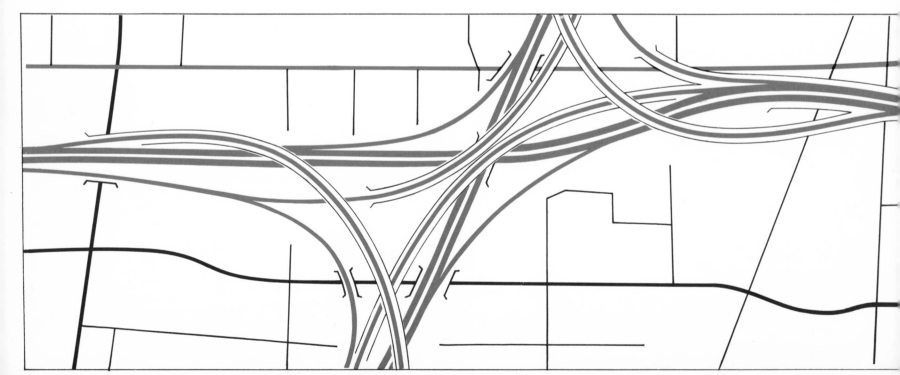

Freeways are also called
turnpikes, expressways,
parkways and thruways.
Many thousands of cars
use these roads every day.

(How many cars can you count on this freeway?)

A street that crosses a freeway must go over it or under it. This crossing is marked like this:

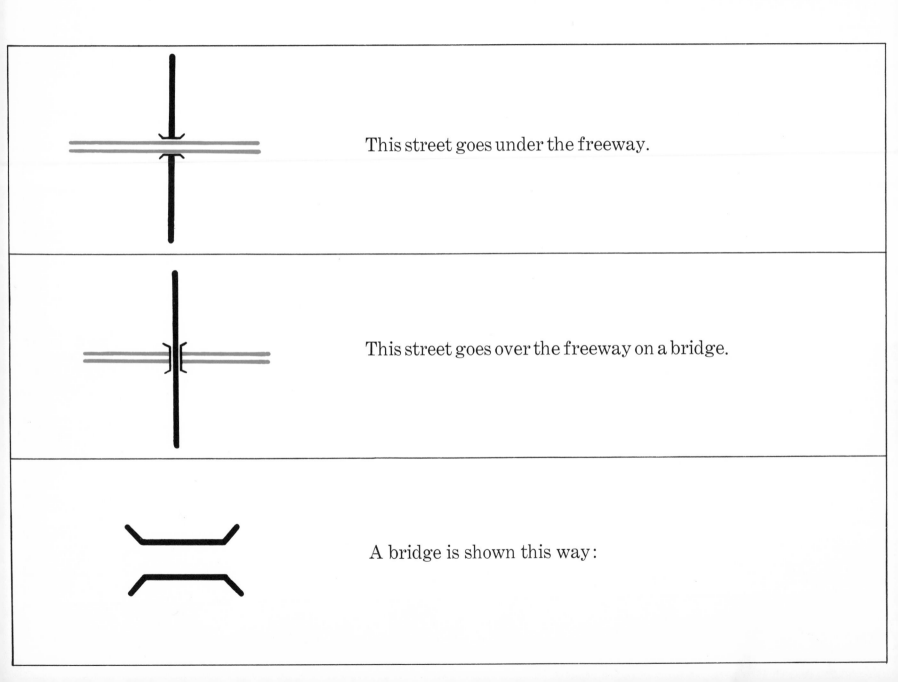

This street goes under the freeway.

This street goes over the freeway on a bridge.

A bridge is shown this way:

Under the freeway.　　　　　　Over the freeway.

Sometimes one freeway goes over another. Here four freeways cross each other in four layers.

This crossing is called a clover leaf because it looks like the shape of a leaf of clover.

The on and off roads are called ramps...on ramps and off ramps.

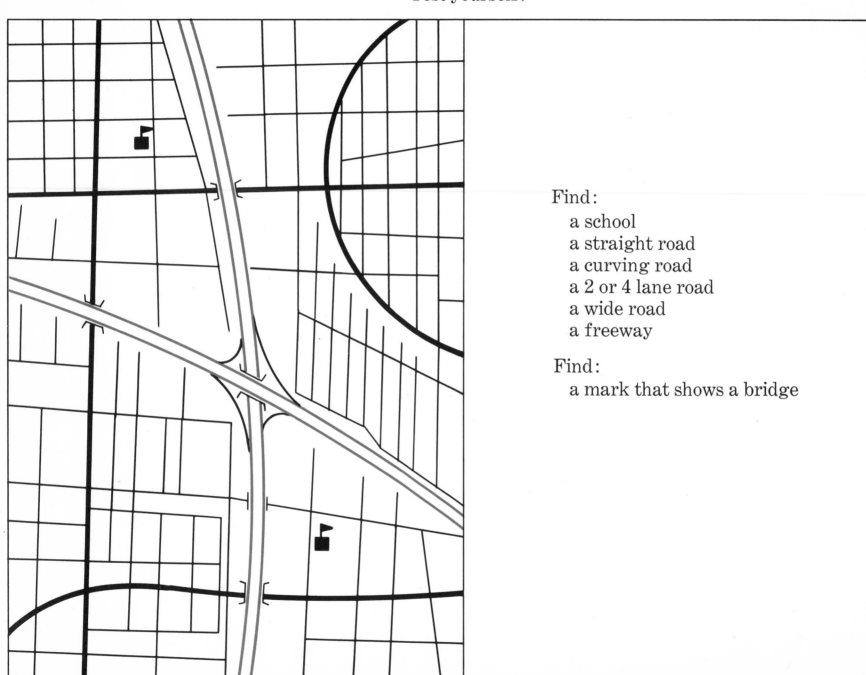

Test yourself:

Find:
- a school
- a straight road
- a curving road
- a 2 or 4 lane road
- a wide road
- a freeway

Find:
- a mark that shows a bridge

Most of the people

using a city map

want to know the location

and direction

of the roads and freeways.

City maps show these

and many more things.

A map can show an airport and the runways on it.

Maps show water in many places. In a lake...

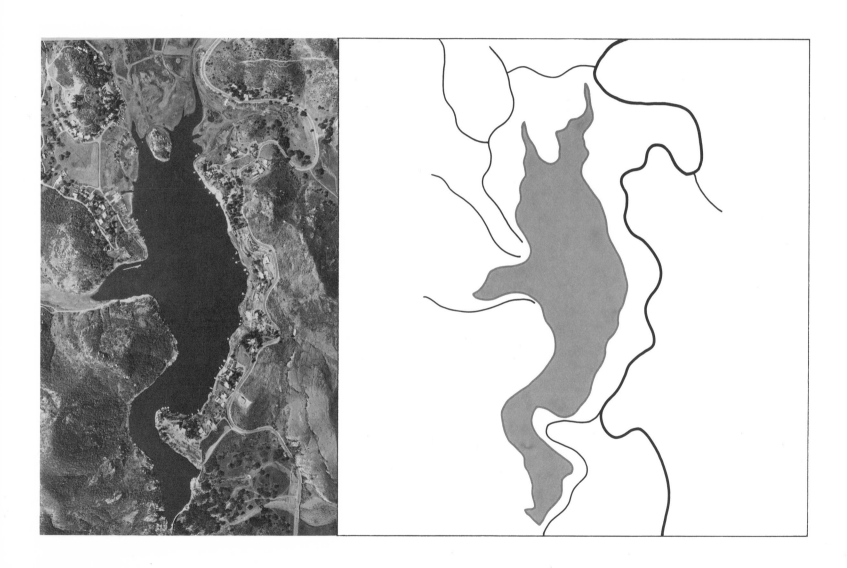

In a man-made lake called a reservoir…

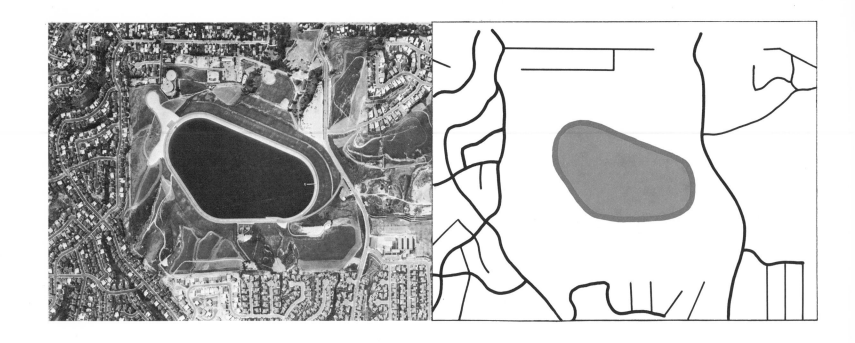

Water is stored in a reservoir.

Water is kept there until it is needed.

The reservoir has to be filled

from a creek, canal or river.

The rivers are shown on maps by blue lines.

Can you find the signs
that show where
bridges cross the river?
Remember?

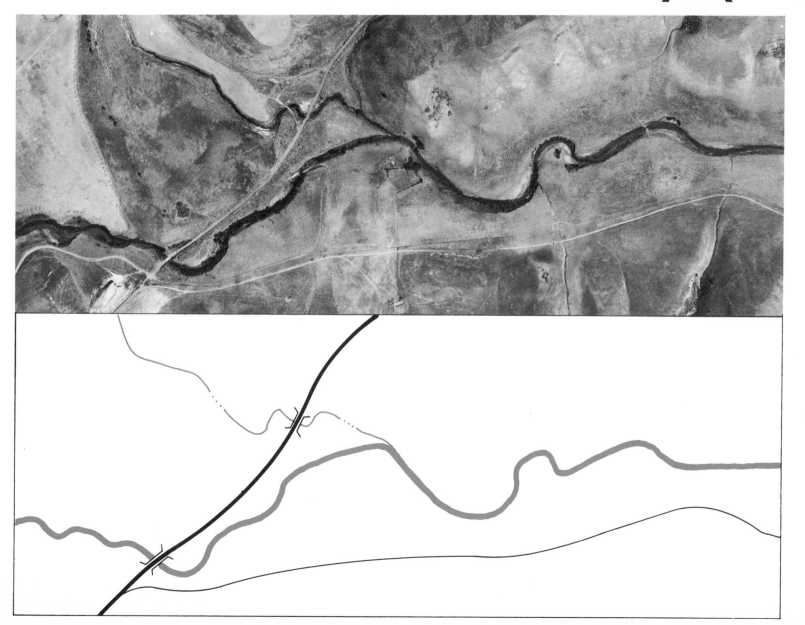

25

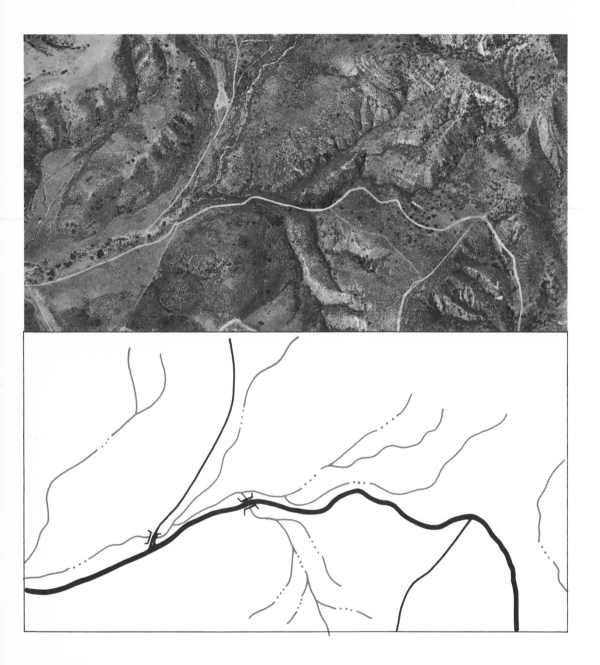

Can you find the creek?
The creeks are marked
with blue lines like this:

A creek is *much*
smaller than a river.
Guess why the creek
lines curve? Right!
Because the creeks
turn and curve.

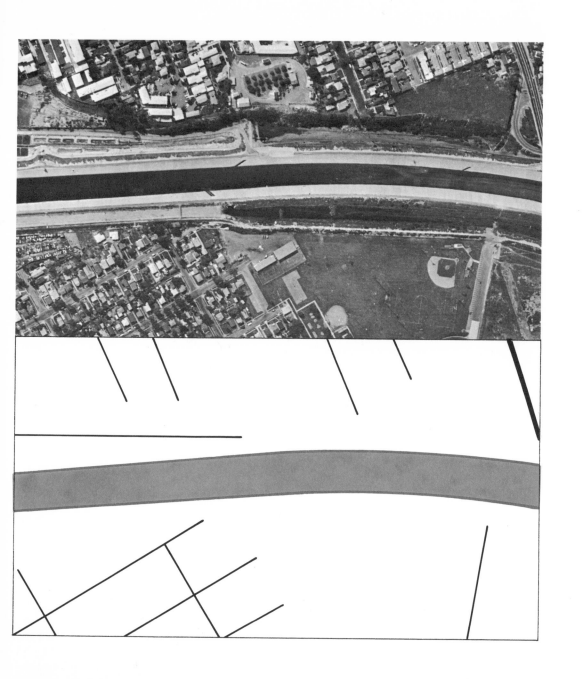

A canal is a large
man-made ditch. It may
be lined with concrete.
It is shown by a single
line or a double line.

It is straighter than a creek.
The canal carries
water from the
reservoir to the city.

27

This city is located by the ocean. The water forms a bay and a harbor.

A bay is a part of an ocean or lake. This map shows the bay and the harbor with the docks.

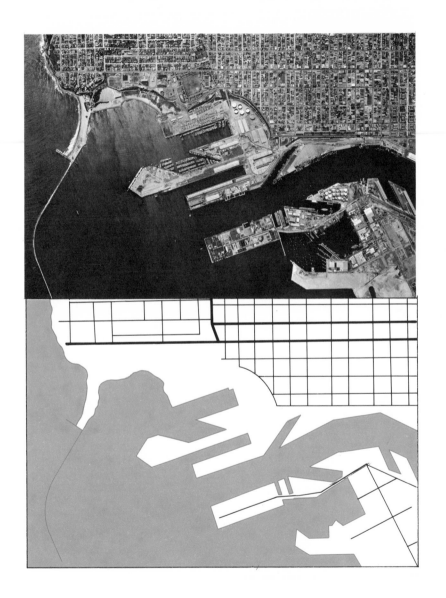

A bay is a part of an ocean or lake. It is partly surrounded by a curve of the shore line.

A harbor is the part of the shore line where ships can anchor. Some harbors are a part of a bay.

(Do you see the ship at dock in the harbor? Can you find the seaplanes in the bay?)

A map can show railroad tracks: This is the symbol. ┼┼┼┼┼┼┼┼┼┼┼┼

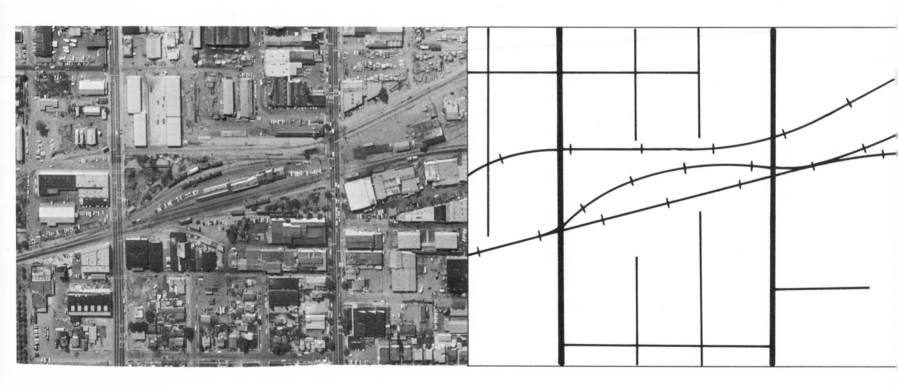

A map can locate a park.

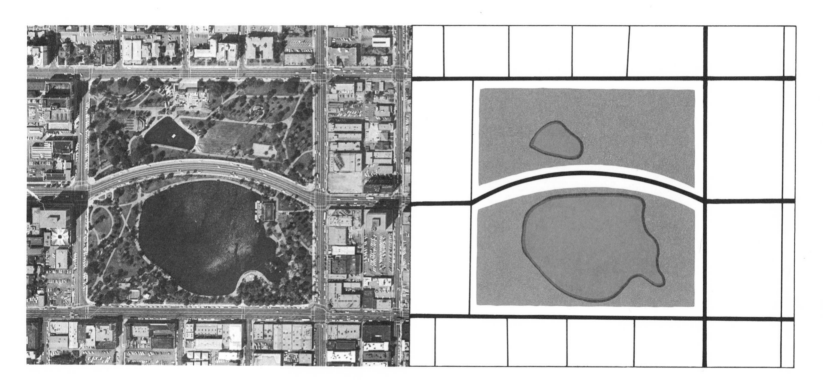

The name of the park and the green color help you find
it. But look carefully. Some maps show parks in other
colors. Some maps that do not use colors show parks
marked with dots.

Maps have signs for many important buildings.

You know that this means school:

The flag symbol means that it is an elementary school.

Black blocks show the high school buildings.

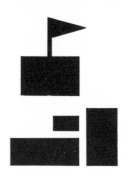

(Can you find a high school?)

32

Maps show other buildings.

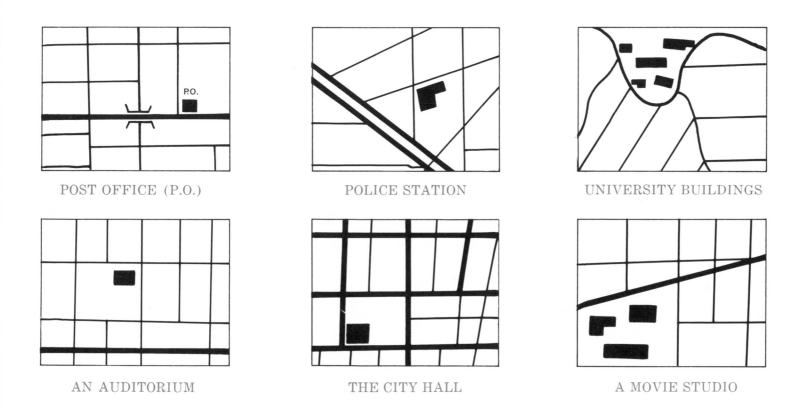

POST OFFICE (P.O.)

POLICE STATION

UNIVERSITY BUILDINGS

AN AUDITORIUM

THE CITY HALL

A MOVIE STUDIO

A map shows where to find streets, parks, waterways, buildings and railroad tracks. To use the map to find these you need to know whether to go . . . .

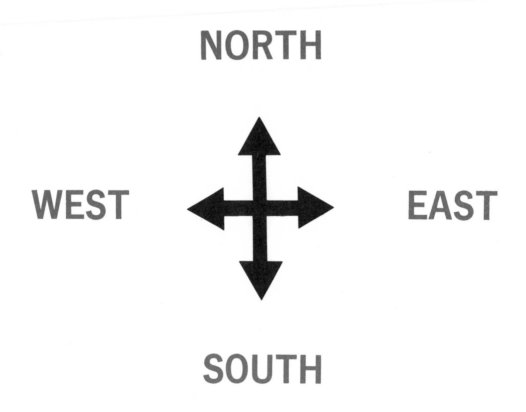

NORTH

WEST   EAST

SOUTH

Maps are made so that the direction North is at the top of the map.

NORTH

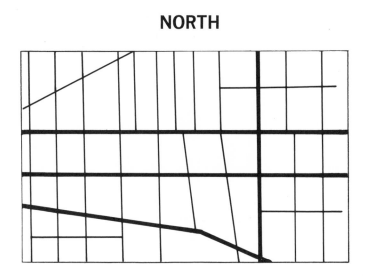

On most maps

there is a sign

to show North.

Sometimes

the sign shows

all four directions.

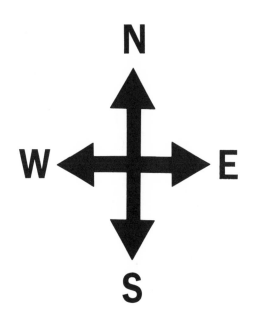

"N" IS FOR NORTH

"S" IS FOR SOUTH

"E" IS FOR EAST

"W" IS FOR WEST

N

S

E

W

These directions are called the four points of the compass.

On some maps the direction-finder sign is made into a
fancy design. This compass design is called a compass rose.

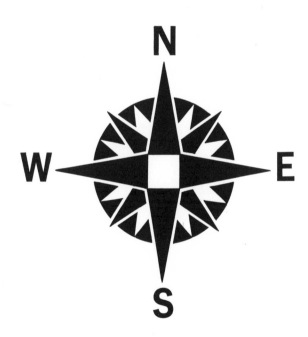

If you know how to read maps
you can find the distance
from one place to another.

You have to know that:

(1) A map shows something
larger made smaller.

(2) A long distance on a road will
be a short distance on a map.

The distance from a school to a
park may be 4 miles. On a map
that distance may be shown by
a line an inch long. |————————|

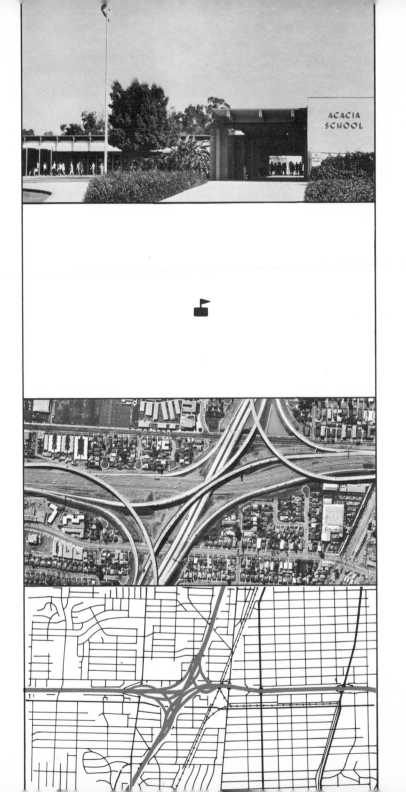

The map maker decides what
distance on the map will equal
a mile. He calls this relationship
a scale of miles.

In the corner of every map is a
drawing of a part of a ruler.
This drawing explains what
measurement on the map equals
a mile. It is called a scale of
miles. This scale of miles shows
that 1 inch on the map is equal
to 4 miles in the city.

A quarter inch equals a mile.
Each map has its own scale
of miles.

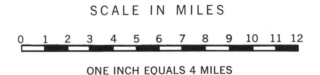

SCALE IN MILES

ONE INCH EQUALS 4 MILES

If you know how to use the $\frac{1}{4}$, $\frac{1}{2}$ and $\frac{3}{4}$ inch marks on a

ruler, you can measure 1 mile, 2 miles and 3 miles on the

map. Every inch you measure on the map will equal four miles.

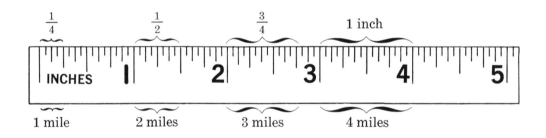

From this school to a park is 3 inches.

1 inch equals 4 miles.

3 inches equals 3x4 miles.

It is 12 miles to the park.

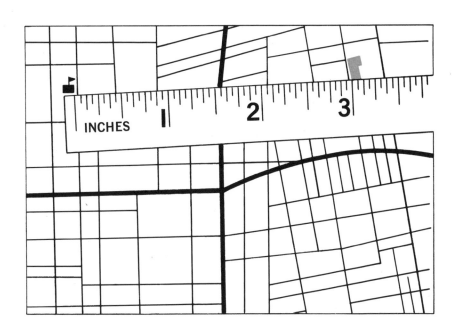

Key to symbols.

——————	REGULAR ROAD
— — — —	STRAIGHT ROAD
∿∿∿	CURVING ROAD
▬▬▬▬	WIDE ROAD
═══════	FREEWAY
⊐⊏	BRIDGE
╋	INTERSECTION
——————	CANAL
∼∼∼	RIVER
∼·∼·∼	CREEK
⌇	HARBOR
┼┼┼┼┼	RAILROAD TRACK

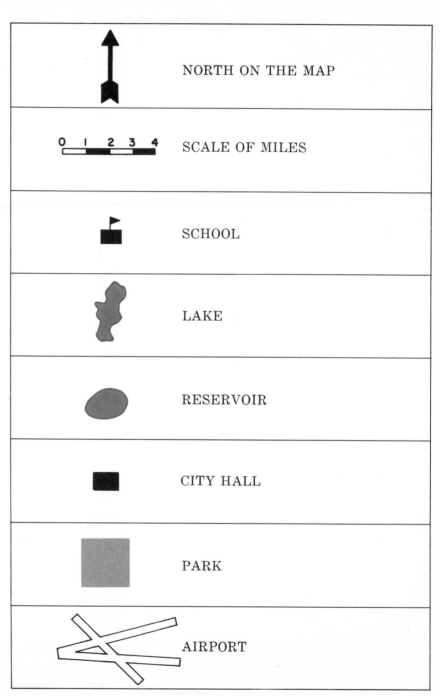

↑	NORTH ON THE MAP
0 1 2 3 4	SCALE OF MILES
⚑	SCHOOL
▮	LAKE
⬭	RESERVOIR
▬	CITY HALL
◼	PARK
✳	AIRPORT

What can you read here?

You can ask for a map
of your town or city at:
a gas station,
your city hall,
the automobile club.

Have a good time reading maps!

GLOSSARY

Intersection	A place where streets or roads cross each other.
Freeways Expressways Turnpikes Parkways Thruways	Names for roads that are especially made so traffic may travel without stopping for intersections. They have no stop signs or traffic lights.
Clover Leaf	A place where the freeways go over or under each other. The curved roads make shapes like clover leaves.
Runways	At an airport, the long flat strips of road used by planes for landings and take-offs.
Reservoir	A man-made lake. It is used as a place to store water.
Creek	A small stream of water, usually narrow and not very deep.
Canal	A man-made ditch dug so that water may run from one place to another. Some canals are large enough to be used by boats. Others are just big enough to bring water to a field or to a pumping station.
Bay	A part of a larger body of water. It is next to the land. The land of the shore curves around 2 or 3 sides of the bay.
Harbor	A bay, or other protected part of the water, where ships come in. They come to docks. Sometimes they anchor in the bay.
Scale	The measured distance on a ruler that stands for distance on a map.